The Cat, The Sun, and The Mirror

First in a Series of
Cool Cat Mysteries

A Story for All Ages

Based on the Ancient Japanese Myth
of Amaterasu, the Sun Goddess

By Robert A. Anderson
and Edward C. Sullivan

Illustrations by Hannah Way Rawe

The Cat, the Sun, and The Mirror

A Cool Cat Mystery

By Robert A. Anderson and Edward C. Sullivan
Illustrations by Hannah Way Rawe

Published by FlashyDame
West Wyoming, PA
catsunmirror@gmail.com

FlashyDame is a division of Libro Gumbo Limbo

coolcatnoir.com
coolcatnoir.tumblr.com

Art Director: Louise Ma

ISBN 978-0-9891895-4-5

Conceived, written, illustrated, printed and bound in the United States of America.

Printed by Llewellyn & McKane, Inc.
31 Hill Street, Wilkes-Barre, PA 18702-4923
www.llewellynmckane.com

"We cats work alone."

— Bucky Katt, in "Get Fuzzy,"
by Darby Conley

This book is dedicated to the ones who came before, to those who also prowled the dark and lonely streets looking for answers, including Lew Archer, Jeff Bailey, Mike Hammer, Philip Marlowe, Sam Spade, and Spenser.

In the myths and tales
of a country named Japan,

The Sun is considered a lady,
not a man.

And then one day,
or so we are told,

This Sun wasn't there—
it was dark and cold!

DINER

Chapter One

Take a city—any city—this one here,
That one there, anywhere:
A place to work, a place to live,
A place to share, a place to give,
In apartments, 'hoods, single-families,
Schools, shops, factories;
A place to live, a place to pray,
Lots of games for all to play.
Up in the morning, to work by nine,
Lunch at noon, waiting in line,
Home in the evening, kids are fine.

You can picture it—right?

Now hear it too: sounds at night,
From theatres, movies, a music club;
From the street, the general hubbub:
Cops in the alley, breaking up fights;
People protesting, demanding
their rights.
The silence of the sky—what a sight!
Stars above: lovers' delight.

And who am I? What do I do?
Just a guy...with a tale for you.
So let's proceed—get on with our story:
A morning came when there was no
more glory.
On the street, folks were not amused—
Were in the dark, confused.

City People

Hey–what's happenin'? Day's begun–

But something's missing–where's the Sun?

This is scary; this can't be right.

Supposed to be day, but it's still night.

Maybe it's an ellipse–it'll be okay.

What're you, stupid? Ellipses don't
last all day.

No sir, and no ma'am—an eclipse
it was not.
What happened, it turned out,
was key to our plot.
The Sun was gone—missing—
that was a fact.
In schools, students were told,
Don't overreact.

Teacher

As for the Sun...she could just be tired.
Perhaps a substitute could be hired.

Little Girl

She could be gone for good!

Teacher

Or...just wearing a hood.

Little Boy

Or behind a mountain, like, hiding–

Little Girl

Or deep in a hole, like, sighing.

Little Boy

I know–she must be in a mine.

Teacher

What kind?

Little Girl

I'll bet it's of silver...or gold–

Little Boy

Or even of coal!

Girls and Boys

Oh, no!

Teacher

Of course it's bad for you and me,
But we must study the ecology.

Little Girl

The birds, the bees, the frogs, the plants–

Little Boy

The elephants–even the ants!

Nothing but nighttime, day after day,
With everyone trying to make it okay,
Figuring out what went wrong,
Looking for answers in reason and song.

City Singer
"You Are My Sunshine–"

City Patrons
Hey you, stop it–
Not another verse!

We can't take it–
It makes it worse!

City Singer
"Blue Moon–"

City Patrons
But we don't have a moon!
Not without our Sun.

Try a different tune–
Sing another one!

City Singer
"Ain't No Sunshine–"

City Patrons
Yeah–that's better!
Let us suffer.

City Singer
"You are my lightbulb, my only lightbulb–"

City Patrons
Yeah! Yeah! Yeah!

No longer did people feel young,
As love songs went unsung
And poets put away their pens;
Preachers spewed constant amens.
Now lovers ceased their strolls,
And marriage bureaus all closed.

But then one day—or night,
who could tell?—
Some people spoke up—it was
time to rebel.

City People

We need someone–

Someone now!

We need someone–

Oh, yeah–

And how!

This can't go on–

Like living in a cave!

We need someone–

Someone who's brave!

I said we need someone–

Like who, like why?

To find the Sun–

Put her back in the sky!

City Man

So–let's have a meeting.

City Woman

Yo–it's already begun!

As people gathered on the floor,
A stranger slipped in through the door.
No one noticed; they were too busy:
Excited—angry—in a tizzy.

City People

I say–

No, I say–

What we need is–

A private eye!

All in favor?

Aye! Aye! Aye!

But wait–what's that?

A private eye?

He hunts for things.

Like, you know, a cat.

What? A cat?

And out of the shadows
stepped just that.

Cool Cat

No problem, folks, you've got your guy.

City People

Hey–who are you?

Where'd you come from?

Cool Cat

Who am I? A private eye.

Chapter Two

A woman there a long glance took,
Then asked the Cat—

City Woman
Are you as cool as you look?
I mean, are you as cool as you seem?
How'd you like a bowl of cream?

Cool Cat
Now listen, princess:
I'll do the asking–see?
To answer is not my business;
Trouble is: I seek it out.
Trouble is what I'm all about.

City Woman
Wow, this private eye is one Cool Cat–
He's got to be, wearin' that hat.

Cool Cat
You got it, sis, but don't forget:
"Private eye" means just that:
About myself I don't chit-chat.

City People
So help us then, Mr. Private Eye,

We need our Sun back in the sky–

And our moon–

We need them soon!

Cool Cat
I think I see
The job laid out for me.
No need to ask;
I'll take the task.

City People
Hey, this is great!

You got that straight!

A private eye first-rate!

Let's celebrate!

They formed a circle, danced
and danced,
Sounding off with many a chant.

City People
EE–AYE–EE–AYE–EE–AYE–AYE–
We have got a private eye!

FEE AND FI AND FO AND FUN–
He is going to find the Sun!

EE–AYE–EE–AYE–EE–AYE–AYE–
We have got a private eye!

FEE AND FI AND FO AND FUN–
He is going to find the Sun!

Meanwhile on a dark
    and lonely city street
Our Cat took a stroll;
    this was more his beat.
By himself the Cat had his own
    tune to hum,
But the song he sang
    was rather glum.

Cool Cat

Well, that is clear:
They love their volunteer.
But if they could see
The real me,
They'd wonder what they've started here.

I didn't lie;
I am a private eye.
But to find the Sun,
Or anyone,
For me, it's a quite a lot to try.

Most things that folks have lost,
These things I've never found.
A missing coat,
A stolen boat,
A garden rake,
A chocolate cake,
A kangaroo
With a green tattoo—
These things got lost,
Remain unfound.
I never was
A hunting hound.

But all that's past;
I'll find the Sun and fast.
She'll shine again.
She'll shine and then
I'll be the people's hero here at last,
At last,
I'll be the people's hero here at last.

Chapter Three

But where could he find her?
Where should he look?
The Cat needed an answer;
He needed a hook.
He wanted to hear the talk,
What people had to say;
So he prowled the Riverwalk,
Went out on Broadway.

City People
You hear what I hear?

Spill it: I'm all ear.

What everyone's sayin':
She didn't get lost, our Lady Sun.

No? Then what did happen?
She's out havin' some fun?

Nah–it was a crime–a snatch.

You mean–?

That's right: kidnap!

So the Cat decided he had to see
The boss of all the bosses, Mister B.
"B" as in big: Mister Bigg, that would be;
The one, the only one,
who wore the crown:
The boss of all the crime in town.
But it wasn't so easy, Cat found out.
First came a bodyguard—
with a big bad snout!

Dog Bodyguard
Arf-arf-arf!

Cool Cat
You barkin' at me?

Dog Bodyguard
I bark, you talk–see?

Cool Cat
I want to see your boss.

Dog Bodyguard
No way, Cat–get lost!

Cool Cat
Tell him I'm here, you ugly cow!

Dog Bodyguard
I'm a dog! And there's no cats allowed!
Get out, or there'll be trouble–I promise.

Cool Cat
Oh, yeah? Trouble is my business.

Dog Bodyguard
You found it, Cat: *GROWL!*
Which means scat!

Cool Cat
Try this, Dog: *HISS!*
Which means take that!

It looked to become quite a fight,
    dog vs. cat,
Till the man himself entered the scene.
He was big, all right—dare I say "fat"?

Mr. Bigg
What's going on here, what's all the noise?
I was taking a nap; I'm a little annoyed.

Cool Cat
Mr. Bigg, I presume.

Dog Bodyguard
You shut up, Cat!

Mr. Bigg
Beat it, Dogface–to your room.

Dog Bodyguard
Aw…I wanted that hat.

Mr. Bigg
So, Mr. Shamus, what's on your mind?

Cool Cat
What's not in the sky–what I'm gonna find.

Mr. Bigg
Lose the riddles, Cat–they're not my style.

Cool Cat
Is that right? I'll put it in your file.

Mr. Bigg
Don't like rhymes either: another one,
    you're out.

Cool Cat
Oh? And you're the bouncer?
    That, I doubt.

Mr. Bigg
That's it! Nails!

Nails
Here, boss.

Mr. Bigg
Lefty!

Lefty
Here, boss.

Mr. Bigg
Moll!

Moll
You called, boss?

Quite a beauty she was, this Moll,
With ruby red lips, and tall.
And so the gang was all there,
Encircling, just like a snare.
But was our Cat afraid—ascared?
Uh-uh: he stayed cool: prepared.

Mr. Bigg
So it's rhymes you want, Mr. Cool?
I can play, I've been to school.
You say you need to talk to me?
What d'you want–a cup of tea?
Or do you want a truck hijacked?
Then I'm your guy, and that's a fact.
'Cause I'm big–

Nails
He's big! He wears the crown–

Lefty
The boss–of all the crime in town.

Mr. Bigg
Pick it up, Moll. Tell Cat what's what.
Without any if, and, or but.

Moll
Sure, Mr. B...
Need a break from being good?
Tired of doing the things you should?
Need to dip your paws in a little vice?
Want to play some back-street dice?
Then see the one who wears the crown–

Mr. Bigg
That's me—I'm big!

Moll
The boss of all the crime in town.

Mr. Bigg
Nails, Lefty!

Nails
Contrast! Contrast!
We got it to sell.
We tell 'em it's heaven,
But they know it's hell.

Lefty
Bad things for good folks—
Now ain't that a shame.
But that's how it is,
In the criminal game.

Moll
So what do you want, Cat—
to have some fun?

Cool Cat
Like I told your boss: I want the Sun.

Mr. Bigg
The Sun?

Cool Cat
That's the one.

Mr. Bigg
Now I see: you're here for ecology.
No prob'—we'll fix you up, one-two-three.
Nails, Lefty—tell him!

Nails
If the government is after you—

Lefty
If the feds are on your trail—

Nails
Say you're dumping toxic goo,
And you're afraid of goin' to jail—

Lefty
If you've got illegal waste,
Garbage that you don't want traced—

Mr. Bigg
Well, I know where it can be placed—

Nails

'Cause he's big! He wears the crown–

Mr. Bigg

The boss–of all the crime in town.
Poison landfill means money to me,
As profitable as sin used to be.

Moll

We can hide it deep in the ground,
Late at night when no one's around.

Nails

'Cause he's big–

Cool Cat

Hold on–that's enough! I want to speak!

Moll

Well, come on, Cat, don't take all week.

Cool Cat

Listen, Mr. Bigg–I'm talking true;
People gossip; they're blaming you.
Say that kidnap's what you've done,
Say you want a ransom for the Sun,
Say that you're the guilty one.

Mr. Bigg
Well, they're just rumors,
  and they ain't right;
I don't need this eternal night.
Used to be, daytime, folks did what's right;
At night what they did was out of sight–

Moll
Then I would feed their appetite.

Mr. Bigg
Day was good, and night was bad.
By day they got rich; at night they got had.

Lefty
Nighttime used to be our time of day,
Our time to lead good people astray.

Nails
But now the Sun is gone, it's always dark;
Now nonstop mugging in every park.

Moll
Sin for anyone at anytime,
And that's not good for organized crime!

Mr. Bigg
You heard her, Cat–
Now hear me, before you scat:
You find the Sun, and find her now!

Cool Cat
That's what I'm doing anyhow.

Nails
Hey–you're working now for Mr. Bigg.

Cool Cat
No way–this here's my personal gig.

Moll
You take chances, Cat–
You're cool...I like that.

Mr. Bigg
Enough! Take a hike, Mr. Private Eye;
You find the Sun–and don't just try!

Chapter Four

Along an alley, a city street,
Again he prowled on padded feet,
Cool Cat—searching for the Sun,
Packing neither knife nor gun,
In a city full of crime,
With darkness all the time,
Darkness, crime, and poverty, too;
All the people with nothing to do.
Electric meters running night and day;
Businesses closing—they couldn't pay.

City Man
Hey–have you heard
The latest word?

City Woman
Another rumor? Which one now?
The sun went off to Curacao?

City Man
No–that it's all a big conspiracy.
Some people are getting rich.

City Woman
You know it isn't me.
So who? What people? Which?

Cool Cat tapped his head;
He heard what was being said.
It was the jet-set crowd,
The power brokers, the proud,
Not the people on the street.
He had to talk to the elite.
But where to start, which one to call?
The house of Major Domo, hidden
by a wall.
Up on it he leapt, then over
to a sycamore;
Down he jumped, then knocked
at the door.

MART
SALE
ng Out of
siness!
SALE
FORECLOSURE
Bank Owned
CLOSED

But it wasn't the Major who came—
    not yet:
First to greet him was
    the Majorette.

Majorette
Well...and who are you?

Cool Cat
Funny–that's my question too....
Ah-hem–I'm a cat, a cool one, a private eye.

Majorette
I can see you're a cat: I've got eyes.
Why come here? You're
    one of those spies?

Cool Cat
I'm hot on a case; this is no disguise.
I'm here to see the Major–
    Domo by name.

Majorette
See my dad? What for?
    What's your game?

Cool Cat
Not a game; it's my work; it never ends.

Majorette
Too bad. I was hoping we'd be friends.
You're kind of cute–for a cat,
From your paws right up to your hat.

What was it Cool Cat felt,
    pulling him close?
Was it the cream he had sipped,
    did he overdose?

Cool Cat
Some other time, maybe, we could...

Majorette
Yes? What?

Cool Cat
Chat.

Just as it seemed
    they might share a kiss,
Enter the father,
    eliciting a—

Cool Cat
Hisssss!

Major Domo

A cat at my door–what's this?

Majorette

He's here, he says, on business.

Major Domo

Then I'll take over, Daughter dear....
I said you can go now–is that clear?

Majorette

Fooey!

Major Domo

Come in, Cat, let's have your chat.
First I'll tell you where I'm at.
And–if you don't mind–
My choice of speech is rhyme.
I'm somewhat of a poet;
My words, I trust, will show it.
Now...Major Domo is my name;
Making money is my game.
A middle man, I make my plan,
To be a go-between.
You see, I am a lobbyist,
In cutting deals, a specialist.
An expert, you know, in making dough,
I am a go-between.
The slickest you've ever seen:
A businessman, but not too crass,
I'm upper, upper middle class.

Cool Cat

I see.

Major Domo

You do? Not everyone does–alas.
Take air pollution–which is a crime.
You fill the air with soot and grime–
But you don't mean to be unclean;
What you need is a go-between.
Enviro laws can be pretty tough,
Eco cops can get quite rough.
I place a gift–you get my drift?–
Your record is wiped clean;
I make you look *sooo* green.

Cool Cat

Then...you know the man–

Major Domo

Who knows *the* man.
My motto is: "Oh yes, I can."
A business tango, it takes three:
There's you, the government, and me.
I lubricate, facilitate,
I tap the tambourine.

Cool Cat

So that's how you go green.

Major Domo

Easy: we meet downtown, the Ritz Hotel;
You tell the tale you want to sell.
To me you give a modest fee.
We're playing ball; I place a call;
A man I pay says, "A-okay."
Now you pollute–who gives a hoot?
The fix is in, it's set, you win–
A richer guy, and so am I.
'Cause I'm your go-between.

Cool Cat
You really know the scene.

Major Domo
I'll only take a small percent–

Cool Cat
You're for sale, you mean–

Major Domo
I prefer to say for rent.
So, Cat, how can I help you?
    Ah-chooo!
Does your chimney smoke,
    make others blue?
Do your trucks asphyxiate
As they ride the interstate–
You need a ticket fixed?

Cool Cat
Well, Major Domo, if I may,
I'll tell you why I'm here today.
The sun is missing, as you know,
While you are busy making dough.
So I've been chosen–I'm the one,
Who's job it is to find the Sun.
A job, by the way, that doesn't pay–

Major Domo
Doesn't pay? How *déclassé*!

Cool Cat
Enough, Domo! I'm speaking plain:
Are you involved in the kidnap plot?
Is it you, your friends, who hope to gain?
You keep her by some beach,
    somewhere hot,
A Carib isle, a spa in Spain,
Where a visit costs quite a lot?
Now listen to me, Major D:
The Sun's for everybody–see?
She's not a prize;
So don't privatize!

Major Domo
Oh, Cat, don't be so mean!
I'm only a go-between.
I don't deserve such sass;
I'm upper, upper middle class.

Cool Cat
I care less about your rank–

Major Domo
You should–all the way to the bank.

Cool Cat
No thanks! It's the people I fight for–

Major Domo
Ah, yes, "the people"–such a bore!
Well, they won't need sunscreen anymore.
No, Cat, your accusations are not right:
I didn't cause this dreadful night;
I miss the Sun like everyone.
But I like your plan–the rich having fun:
We'll pick a spot, call it..."Club Sun."
So bring her back, that's the key
To make a fortune, you and me!

Cool Cat

Your words make me sick and tired.

Major Domo

Then get out–scat–you're fired!
Ah-chooo!
Can't work with a cat in any case:
There'll be cat hair all over the place.

No sooner had the Major left the room
Than his daughter reentered, abloom.

Majorette

Wait–don't leave–not yet!

Cool Cat

What is it, Majorette?

Majorette

I want to join you in your quest.

Cool Cat

I work alone; I find it's best.

Majorette

But I can help–I've got a computer.

Cool Cat

Oh, yeah? Well, isn't that super.
Sorry, sister, don't mean to snipe,
But I've never been the high-tech type.

Majorette

Get with it, Cat, you don't know what's up.

Cool Cat

I know the Sun isn't; I know I'm tough.

Majorette

But...I need a goal, a mission...
I feel a passion–

Cool Cat

I feel it too...but I'm a loner–
old-fashioned.

And so our Cat took his leave,
Causing the Majorette to bereave.

Majorette

Goodbye, goodbye, my worthy friend,
I hope you find success, in the end.

Only by himself, cast out,
Would Cat reveal his doubt.

Cool Cat

Am I really the one
To find our Lady Sun?
I ask but no reply;
All I do is sigh.
I think I'm tough–
But tough enough?
I've got to give another try!

Chapter Five

So now along the boulevard
Cool Cat prowled, listening hard.

City People

Heard the latest?

Which latest?

The latest latest.

Oh, that latest.

It's the Ocean, see?

Huh? The Ocean is the sea.

That's right.

What's right?

You're right, see?

I'm confused.

Don't be.

The people somehow
got the notion
Sister Sun was grabbed by
Brother Ocean,
Who had always been
jealous of the Sun.
So out of seaweed he made a huge net,
And then, as morning had just begun,
The moon having already set,
She started to fly across the sky,
When he threw the net—
got her—bye-bye!

City Man

Now I get it–the Ocean, the sea–I see!

Our private eye had always learned
To leave no clue or hint unturned.
So, though cats don't like to swim,
He felt this rumor gripping him.
He took a great big breath of air—
And dove deep down, into *la mer.*

Dogfish

Arf-arf-arf! Who goes there?

Cool Cat

Oh, no–a dog?! Way down here?

Dogfish

Dogfish–to you. Now beat it, creeper.

Cool Cat

Will do–deeper and deeper.

As he said, the Cat kept going down,
Till the Lord of the Sea he finally found.

Ocean

Welcome, Mr. Cat, make yourself at home.
My, my, how far you do roam!
May I ask: why do you call?
Why bother to come here at all?

Cool Cat

I'm looking for your sis–
she's disappeared.

Ocean

Go ahead and look–
but she's not down here.

Cool Cat

No? With her gone, you'd be number one:
A much bigger Ocean, without the Sun.

Ocean

Well, it's better for me, I must confess,
With my waters drying much, much less.
Soon, I figure, I'll no longer be
Simply known as Lord of the Sea.

Cool Cat

No? What's the game, then?
What's your call?

Ocean

Why, I'll flood the world–
I'll be Lord of All!

Cool Cat

I knew it: with Sun away, no evaporation,
Ocean grows and grows–an inundation!

Ocean

Yes, yes–I'll splash where
never I could;
My waves will seep into
every neighborhood.
My creatures will be able
to creep and crawl
Into more and more places–
they'll have a ball!
You, Shark–
what will be your beat?

Shark

What do you think?
We sharks want Wall Street.

Ocean

And you, Mr. Octopus,
with your many arms?

Octopus

Times Square we'll pick–
with its many charms.

Ocean

I can tell Ms. Oyster
has a preference too.

Oyster

We're more upscale–
Upper East Side will do.

Ocean

What say you, Whale,
now the world's all dark?

Whale

We need lots of room–
how about Central Park?

Ocean

Monkfish, pray tell
what you anticipate.

Monkfish

The mountains, Master:
better to meditate.

Ocean

There you have it, Cat, what's on our mind.
There'll be no receding of waters this time.
So forget about hopping onto any ark–
Hoping after forty days to disembark.
As for animals, long ago
they came from the sea–
So grow some gills, Cat,
a catfish you can be.

Dogfish

Can't wait, Cat: we'll have some
good fights.

Sunfish

We sunfish will provide the lights!

Cool Cat

But...but...how about people–humans?
Babies, girls, boys, men, women?

Ocean

For them, I'm afraid, we'll not shed a tear;
They use and abuse us sorely down here.
In their ways, they're quite devilish;
Consider this: how much they overfish,
Catching more than they need for lunch.
The people? All in all a nasty bunch.

Cool Cat

Uh-oh...I'm beginning to feel a little sick.

Ocean

Go up and take a breath–be quick!

The watery creatures all lined up—
Cod, haddock, flounder, scup—
To salute and wave to the private eye,
Give him a proper briny goodbye.

Cod

Bye, bye, Cool Cat, and cheerio!

Haddock

Tell folks we're coming–to say hello!

Flounder

Things are going to be changing, bro!

Scup

Soon midtown'll be an archipelago!

Chapter Six

The Cat came back sore and depressed.
He was tired; he needed a rest.
No longer did he have a clue;
He didn't know what to do.
Wandering through the city dark,
He found himself in an offbeat park.
A bunch of dogs were
    hanging around,
Some awake, some asleep
    on the ground,
Warming themselves
    by a barrel of flame,
Of different breeds,
    but really the same.

First Dog
Hey guys, look who it is.

Second Dog
Bow-wow. If we weren't so tired–
Dog-tired–we'd give you the biz.

Cool Cat
If I wasn't so cat-tired, I'd give you a hiss.

Third Dog
But now, without the Sun,
Life has lost all its fun.

First Dog
Hey, look who's coming now.

Second Dog
It's Old Dog–bow-wow-wow.

Third Dog
Are you kidding? We're all old now.

But this old dog did seem different,
With a hidden kind of merriment.
Nearing the Cat, he moved quite slow,
Keeping the pace of life's new flow.

Old Dog
Pleased to meet you, Mr. Private Eye.
Come to get a little shut-eye?
You are Cool Cat, are you not?

Cool Cat
I can see you're hip to the plot.

Old Dog
Ah yes, I've followed your quest,
And it seems to me that at best
You've gotten nowhere–
meaning, right here.

Cool Cat
Right again, Old Dog;
you've got a big ear.

Old Dog
Don't be sore, Cat;
don't get me wrong.
But aren't you always singing
another's song?

Cool Cat
You're getting too nosy, old guy.
Don't forget, I'm a private eye.
I don't answer questions; I ask them.
That's my style; I solve the problem.
So take your advice to a different cat;
On me your words are falling flat.

Old Dog
Ah yes, you're known for being cool.
But aren't you being now a furry fool?
Answers aren't somewhere out there.

Cool Cat
No? Okay, Old Dog, tell me where.

Old Dog
They're inside you, that's where to look.

Cool Cat
Inside–?

Old Dog
You'll find a mysterious book.

Cool Cat
I don't have time to read;
A clue is what I need.

Old Dog
Listen, Cool Cat, I'm giving you one:
Inside you, there you'll find the Sun.

Cool Cat
What? That doesn't make sense.

Old Dog
Yes, yes, we're all a little dense.

Cool Cat
Hey! Stop talking nonsense!

Old Dog
Sense? Nonsense?
What's the difference?

Cool Cat
All right, Old Dog, enough of your riddle.
I don't have time to fiddle and diddle.

Old Dog
Then I'll tell you straight, Mr. Cool Cat:
If you want this, then search for that.
Opposites–they're where it's at.
When looking for light,
search where it's dark–
Like finding that fire
here in this park.
Within you is the mirror–

Cool Cat
"The mirror"? "Within"?

Old Dog
Where you'll find your twin–

Cool Cat
There's only me, no other!

Old Dog
Of course there is: a yang for every yin.
In the mirror you'll find it, you'll see.
Who knows, Cat–it could even be me!

Cool Cat
But how–?

Old Dog
Could it be?
Dog, cat–they're only forms, the outer.
Know the inner–yourself, the Sun–
Know all about her!

Cool Cat
I find no help in your forced rhyme;
I tell you I'm running out of time.

Old Dog
There's time enough; there always is.
My advice? Take a break from your biz.

Cool Cat
No way–I'm going ahead; I can't slack.

Old Dog
Just the opposite: you should go back.

Cool Cat

Back to where? What are you saying?

Old Dog

You need to return: to the beginning.
It's a journey we all must wend
If we are ever to find our end.
Remember my words: within, go deep.
Now, Cat, how about a little sleep?

And then Old Dog went on his way,
Leaving our Cat with nothing to say.
But to himself he pondered,
As around the city he wandered.

Cool Cat

Inside of me
I keep my mystery.
I don't reveal
The way I feel:
I hide it,
Every bit.

By a spot that seemed secure
He curled up, cat-like, not sure
Whether he was resting or sleeping,
As his words kept repeating—

Cool Cat

Inside of me...
Mystery...
Don't reveal...
Way I feel...
Mystery...
Inside me...
Mystery...
Mirror...
Other...
The twin...
Within...

Chapter Seven

As the Cat lay still, out of it,
Look who came to pay a visit.
To the private eye they were not kind,
One by one, him they maligned.

Mr. Bigg
Hey, Cat–you find the Sun yet?
Gonna run for help to the Majorette?

Ocean
Look at yourself, Cat–what a mess!
Can't find the answer–not even a guess.

Major Domo
No answer–but more important–no dough.
And he thinks he's so macho.

The Majorette, as if on a mission,
Came by too, but not to dis him.
She set up her laptop, seeming to focus
On some high-tech hocus-pocus—
When suddenly the Cat leapt up
With all the pep of a little pup.
But wait—Cat was still on the ground
While this other was running around.

Cool Cat
What's your name?–I know we've met.
Wait, I know–Nanette?

Majorette
No!

Cool Cat
Babette?

Majorette
No!

Cool Cat
Paulette?

Majorette
No!

Cool Cat
Yvette?

Majorette
No!

Cool Cat
I'll get it, don't fret–

Majorette
Try the Majorette!

Cool Cat
You must have a twin–right?

Majorette
I don't know–I might.
Who knows? Maybe it's you.

Cool Cat
Forget it–you can't mew.
I've got to find mine–where to look?
In the street? Up a tree? In a book?

Majorette
How about a mirror? I've got one here.

Cool Cat
Where?

Majorette
My computer–now stare.

Cool Cat
The mirror is the screen?

Majorette
It's where the mirror can be seen.

So stare the Cat did
As into the screen he slid.

Cool Cat
But…it's me inside–it's scary!

Majorette
Very scary–but necessary.

Cat saw a light deep in a holy cave;
He told himself: you must be brave!
Then a mirror, tall and bright,
That was shining in the light.
As Cat crept close, he looked inside,
And saw himself in all his pride—

Cool Cat
But the me I see is different from before:
This one has no doubts, is able to soar.

Suddenly he awoke!
It was all a dream, he knew,
Yet it gave him a vital clue.
To himself he spoke.

Cool Cat
Now I know the help I need!

To Major Domo's he flew with speed.

Chapter Eight

Majorette

It's Cool Cat! Like, wow.
Why're you here–like, now?
I know–my daddy you came to see.

Cool Cat

No: it's you, Majorette–

Majorette

Me?

For a moment they smiled, each to each;
For a moment there was no need
for speech.
Then—

Cool Cat

I had a dream–I've seen the light.

Majorette

Awesome, Cat–you're outta sight!

Cool Cat

For the ways of the street, I have a knack,
But computer cred, I totally lack.
So I need you–and your machine.

Majorette

It's here–let's do it–I'm keen!

Over the screen they bent,
Full of purpose, intent.

Majorette

Oh, my Computer—help us find the Sun!
You know all—when all is said and done.

Cool Cat

Yeah, Computer—time is running out.
You can help us; now I have no doubt.

Majorette

First—let's Google "Cool Cat"—your name,
my sweet—
Just to see what it answers...

Cool Cat

"Incomplete"??!!

Majorette

Let's go on... I know—let's Google "Sun."
"No more matches"—that's no fun!

Cool Cat

Take it easy, Majorette—behave.
Now try this one—"cave."

Majorette
"Cave"? It's done.... Wow, look at that–
A hundred million–enough, Cool Cat?

Cool Cat
When looking for light, search in the dark–

Majorette
What?

Cool Cat
It's what Old Dog taught me, in the park.

Majorette
Then...of all the caves, which has the Sun?

Cool Cat
It's got to be the biggest, darkest one.

Majorette
That's all I need–I'll punch it in.
"Biggest..."

Cool Cat
Hey Maje–you think I'm your twin?

Majorette
What?!?

Cool Cat
Nothing.

Majorette
Look–there it is! And not too far from here.

Cool Cat
Let's go–time to make the Sun re-appear.

Majorette
I'm with you! Our goal is set–

Cool Cat
Wait!

Majorette
What for?

Cool Cat
Something I've got to get.

Biggest Caves...

Chapter Nine

The Cat rushed off—
  to where who knew?—
When a cell phone rang—

Majorette

Yes, Daddy, it's true;
It's something I simply have to do.
I know, it isn't what you planned for me.
But...but...how can I make you see?

To explain would take too long;
Instead she sang her song.

Majorette

He's the special someone
I have been waiting for.
Though I never knew him
Till he knocked on my door.
Now I think and think about him,
All of the while,
There's something special in his smile.

There is something special
When he looks in my eyes.
It is kind of dangerous
But still kind of wise.
And he walks and talks with this
Impossible style,
There's something special in his smile.

I see the two of us,
Walking on the boulevard,
Though other people are near,
There are the two of us,
Talking on the boulevard,
Those other people–
We just don't hear them.

There is something special
When he gives me his hand.
Like as if it's something
That the two of us planned.
If I live forever, I am
Certain that I'll
See something special in his smile.

This is a Cat who said
He won't live in darkness,
He'll make the Sun shine again.
If I can help him bring
The world out of darkness
He will be happy then,
We will be happy then.

It's plain to see he's
Something special to me.
I want to be
Wherever he wants to be.
I will walk beside him down the
Longest mile,
There's something special in his smile,
There's something special in his smile.

Meanwhile our private eye was out
In the city, searching about,

Till he found what he was looking for:
"The biggest and the best"
    —Ace Mirror Store.
He bought the largest in the place,
Then carried it back at a rapid pace.

Majorette
Cool Cat, you're back! But a mirror?
It's so big—what's it for?

Cool Cat
Now I know: the Sun's like me—

Majorette
Like you?

Cool Cat
She's lonely. You'll see.
That cave you found—let's go.

Majorette
I'm with you all the way, bro.

So they climbed up the mountain,
Searching for the cave, the biggest one;
When they found it, Cat looked in,
Hoping to find our missing Sun.

Chapter Ten

Cool Cat

Hey, Sister Sun—what's happening?

Lady Sun

Nothing in here—I'm hiding.

Cool Cat

Come out and shine—we need the day.

Lady Sun

You don't need me—now go away.

Cool Cat

But we're tired of constant night;
We want you back—you and your light.

But Lady Sun would not come out.
She told him why, flat-out.

Lady Sun

You people block me
  with smog and smoke.
You don't care; you think
  I'm just a joke.
The ozone is so wasted by your
  poison haze,
That people actually fear
  my shiny rays.
Winter, spring, summer, fall,
You all hang out in the mall.
You'd rather have electric light;
Well, now you've got it, day and night.

Cool Cat

But...but...we'll be better–we'll try.

Lady Sun

Forget it. So long, Cat–bye, bye.

The Cat went back to the Majorette.
Had he given up? Not yet.

Majorette

What's the plan, Cool Cat–fill me in.
I know you have one–by your grin.

The Cat proceeded to do just that,
Then back to the cave he scat.

Cool Cat
Listen, please, Lady Sun, before I go
I need a favor; please, don't say no.

Lady Sun
A favor? What for? Tell me first.
I warn you: I will not be coerced.

Cool Cat
Well...we've decided to have a new Sun–

Lady Sun
You what?!?

Cool Cat
And I ask: did we pick the right one?

Lady Sun
I'm not leaving my little nook.

Cool Cat
No, no, just a quick look.

Lady Sun
Is she pretty?

Cool Cat
Very–some say more than you–
And shines brilliantly too.

Lady Sun
More beautiful than me?
Well...I don't know...let me see.

She did—and as the Sun peeked out
The Majorette turned the mirror about.

Lady Sun
Oh, my, such a pretty one!

Cool Cat
Come closer–meet our new Sun.

Now in the glass the Sun could see
The loveliness that was she.

Lady Sun
But this isn't another–that face is my own;
The beauty I see there is mine alone.

She smiled and felt a sense of pride,
And took another step outside.
Meanwhile a rock Cat rolled to her door,
Wedging it in—she could enter no more.

Lady Sun
But–what have you done, Cat?

Cool Cat
Your hide-out–I've put an end to that!

Lady Sun looked up at the sky
And bid the cave good-bye.
She leaped up high into the blue,
Doing what she was meant to do.
After resuming her rightful place,
A huge smile consumed her face.
And as she filled the world with light,
She sang her song, her eyes so bright.

Lady Sun
To shine again!
To fly the sky and then
To rest the night,
Then light my light
And fly the morning
Sky again!

I love to shine
And all the world is mine.
There down below
The people know
I'll keep them warmer
As I shine.

I'm bright as I can be,
I light up field and tree.
My sun rays beam
On every stream,
The oceans warm,
The rain clouds form,
The flowers grow.
Evaporation's
Good, you know.

Now watch me fly,
I'll race across the sky,
And I will stay
Here every day
And keep on shining, shining
As I fly,
I fly,
I fly.

And Then ...

Cool Cat
Majorette, now that we're done–

Majorette
"Done"? You mean–?

Cool Cat
Just that we've found the Sun.

Majorette
Oh…then…you're going to split?

Cool Cat
No, no, just a question…

Majorette
Say it.

Cool Cat
Well…do you think I'm "incomplete"?

Majorette
No way! I think you're neat.

The End

Acknowledgments

Many thanks go to Patricia Di Benedetto Snyder and Ed. Lange, who displayed such rich artistry and imagination in their staging of the musical version of *The Cat, the Sun, and the Mirror*, Troy, New York, June 2006. Naomi Baker, professor of theatre at Wilkes University, did the same for the revised version, which she directed in Forty Fort, Pennsylvania, July 2011.

Many thanks to digital sweetener extraordinaire Genevieve Hanson for her masterful work in bringing the illustrations to their full, colorful potential. Thank you Goran Krstic and Daniele Frazier; and a special "thank you" to Claus, the cat, and to Scarlet, his cousin, for endless inspiration.

We want to thank Robert Genito for his early support and heartfelt enthusiasm for both the text and illustrations. And thanks to you, too, Big Rose, for helping out in the many readings, both public and private, that nurtured and ripened the manuscript. Without those audiences—in living rooms, an art gallery, a public library, a farmers' market—this book would not have come into existence, and so we cannot forget the hosts and facilitators for those readings, including Nancy and Dave Anderson, Arthur Bennett, Susan and Don DeFlavis, John and Patti Fager, Anthony Ferro, Tom and Leslie Goldstein, Anna Hopkins, Jane and Wilf Innerd, Jill Israel and Billy Karp, Arlene and Don Parsons, and John Roberts.

Louise Ma—what a wonderful job of laying out this manuscript you have done! And Barbara Dauria, thank you so much for your invaluable assistance in getting this book "out there."

And thank you, Vinny Lovegrove, wherever you are.

Robert A. Anderson is a novelist—*Cooks & Bakers* and *Service for the Dead*, both about the Vietnam War, in which he served as a Marine Corps infantry lieutenant—playwright, editor, and teacher of *qigong* and *taiji quan*.

Regarding the inspiration behind *The Cat, the Sun, and the Mirror*, he reflects:

"What is a myth? The ancient Greek statesman and leader Solon wrote: 'Myth is not about something that never happened, it is about something that happens over and over again.' Gregory Nagy, a Greek scholar and former teacher of mine, said, 'Myth is society's way of telling the truth about itself.'

"I'm not sure when I first became acquainted with Japanese mythology and the story of the sun goddess Amaterasu, the myth on which this book is based, but when I did, I began to wonder: what is our American mythology? Do we have one? One day I had a thought: Isn't the private detective, in a sense, a mythic hero? I've always been a big fan of mystery novels, especially detective ones. It seems to me that the private eye is the archetypical loner caught up in the search for the truth. But what is that truth? The solution to the mystery, or the truth about ourselves?

"Every day we look in the mirror: to see what we look like (as if we didn't know). Are we trying to get a better look at ourselves, or are we trying to see what's inside?"

Composer and lyricist, Edward C. Sullivan attended the Sorbonne in Paris and graduated from the New School University in New York City. Fluent in French and a resident of the city since 1957, he taught English as a Second Language for fifteen years at New York University, City University, and other institutions. For Sullivan, language is a key to understanding, to communication, and to education. His passion for education led him to activism and advocacy—and a successful run for the New York State Assembly in 1976. After twenty-five years in the Assembly, including the chair of the Higher Education Committee where he championed the place of higher education in a civil society, while maintaining an unwavering passion to do the right thing, Sullivan retired from the state legislature. His unabashed love for New York City remains undiminished, and in retirement he has returned to write and compose for the theatre—one of his earliest loves. For the musical version of *The Cat, the Sun, and the Mirror*, performed by the New York State Theatre Institute in their 2005-2006 season, he wrote both the lyrics and a highly acclaimed jazz score.

Hannah Way Rawe is a graduate of The Cooper Union School of Art in New York where she shared highest honors with Louise Ma. In fact they were both so brilliant that the school will soon be renamed the Rawe Ma School of Art, or the Ma Rawe School—whichever is decided is easier to pronounce. Ms. Rawe's hobbies include dabbling in designer ice cream and getting lost. If anyone should happen to find her, please return her to Brooklyn, where she sometimes lives (when not in Hawaii, Paris, Amsterdam, or Berlin).

Since early childhood, Louise Ma has been preoccupied with writing, drawing, fitting words and pictures neatly together, and playing good songs over and over again.

coolcatnoir.com